# Heroic Living

## Claiming God's Power

Sharilyn Searls Adair

Abingdon Press / Nashville

**HEROIC LIVING:**
**Claiming God's Power**
by Sherilyn Searls Adair

Copyright © 2004 by Abingdon Press

This book is printed on acid-free, elemental chlorine-free paper.

ISBN 0-687-03651-8

MANUFACTURED IN THE UNITED STATES OF AMERICA
04 05 06 07 08 09 10 11 12 13—10 9 8 7 6 5 4 3 2 1

# Table of Contents

# About the Writer

Sharilyn Searls Adair has served at The United Methodist Publishing House as editor of youth publications, editor of youth and adult publications, staff trainer for church school publications, executive editor of children's publications, and senior editor of Vacation Bible School resources. Since retiring from UMPH in 1996, she has continued to write and edit children's curriculum and to train writers. She has had two children's books published by Abingdon: *Zacchaeus Has a Good Day* and *Where Is Jesus?*

Shari and her husband, Jim, built their own home where they live with three cats. She is an avid recycler and a friend of the planet. Shari says she *adores* pigs.

# A Word of Welcome

Welcome to *Heroic Living: Claiming God's Power*. This five-session Bible study will introduce you to several biblical stories that explore what it means to live a heroic life as a contemporary follower of Jesus Christ. How does the Bible present heroic virtues? What can we learn from the biblical people who demonstrate such virtues? How does heroic living in the Bible compare or contrast with heroic living in contemporary life? How can we practice biblical models of heroic living in contemporary life, even when they might stand in contrast to popular ideas of heroic living? How can we claim God's power as we find ways to practice such virtues in contemporary life?

The story of Daniel promotes and celebrates the heroic virtues of obedience to God alone and of living one's obedience through practices of faith, even in the midst of adversity (Daniel 6). The story of Esther emphasizes heroism as a calling to make right choices in current circumstances. Esther was called to be loyal to the very community that had equipped her to respond to such a calling (the Book of Esther). Four friends who brought a paralyzed man to Jesus for healing were members of a compassionate community. Their determination to help their friend in spite of obstacles was fueled by their faith in Jesus as a healer (Mark 2:1-12). Jesus understood that a poor widow's gift to the temple treasury was motivated by a generous heart that enabled her to give in a spirit of selflessness in spite of her hardships (Luke 21:1-4). Jesus taught his followers that the prerequisite for heroic discipleship is a humble spirit and a contrite heart (John 13:1-17). In all these stories, the view of the hero stands over and against popular perceptions.

## A Few Tips on This Resource

*Heroic Living: Claiming God's Power* is suitable for an intergenerational teaching setting, such as Vacation Bible School, which may meet for two hours or more, or for a 45–60-minute study session on Sunday morning or during the middle of the week. This small-group Bible study offers the opportunity for adults to learn together and for adults, youth, and children to learn from one another. The sessions encourage leaders and learners to try some new teaching and learning styles, to learn in an intergenerational setting, to consider how the Scriptures inform daily life as a disciple of Jesus Christ.

The leader/learner helps in *Heroic Living* meet a variety of learning styles and needs. These helps are designed to generate reflection and discussion, to provide opportunities for faith development through Bible study and group interaction, and to make connections between the Bible and contemporary life. Sessions include opening and closing worship activities and suggestions for intergenerational activities. For ease of use, the leader/learner helps are placed in boxes located near to the relevant main text material.

*Heroic Living* offers many opportunities for you to discover the value of living in relationship with God and for claiming God's power to live as a committed Christian. Our prayer is that you delight in the wonder of heroic living as demonstrated in Scripture and as empowered by God in the world and in your life.

Enjoy!

# Daniel:
# The Importance of Spiritual Disciplines

**Focus:** The story of Daniel promotes and celebrates the heroic virtues of obedience to God alone and of living one's obedience through practices of faith, even in the midst of adversity.

### Opening Moments

Display the words to 1 Corinthians 16:13-14 throughout this entire study either on a large sheet of posterboard or on a chalkboard. Use this verse as a group greeting when you begin each session. Quickly divide into five clusters (individuals, pairs, or small groups depending on your numbers) for the reading. Each cluster in turn is to stand and read one of the phrases beginning with a verb. Read with conviction. Encourage your companions to do what your phrase dictates. Remain standing so that the entire group is standing as the reading ends.

*"Keep alert, stand firm in your faith, be courageous, be strong. Let all that you do be done in love." (1 Corinthians 16:13-14)*

Pray the following prayer:
God of grace and wisdom, God of love and power, we want to learn to live heroically for you. As we engage in this study and as we carry our learning into the world, help us to be alert, to be vigilantly attentive and mentally responsive to the needs and cares of the world around us. Help us to stand firm in the faith that is your gift to us, never wavering in our resolve to do your will. Give us courage and strength to live out that faith in our daily surroundings; and above all help us to love abundantly, claiming your power to make the world better for all whom we encounter. Help us to live as heroes for you in our place and in our time. In Jesus' name. Amen.

## What Is a Hero?

In an essay written in 1958 called "The Decline of Heroes," Arthur M. Schlesinger, Jr., humanities and history professor and adviser to two U.S. presidents, lamented the fact that there were no longer great people of the caliber the world had seen in previous decades. He mentioned personalities such as Woodrow Wilson, Franklin Roosevelt, Winston Churchill, Joseph Stalin, Adolph Hitler, Mohandas Gandhi, Albert Einstein, Sigmund Freud, and Sun Yat-sen. "Some of these great men," he wrote, "influenced the world for good, others for evil; but whether for good or for evil, the fact that each had not died at birth made a difference, one believed, to everyone who lived after them." Schlesinger equated greatness with heroism; and in this essay, he postulated that the capacity for such greatness resides in each individual and that individuals can make a difference in the world. "That there are no indispensable individuals is a fallacy," he wrote. "Individuals have lived who did what no substitute could have done."[1]

As Christians, citizens of God's kingdom in the world, we have different measures for heroism than some of those that Schlesinger lifted up; but his affirmation of the importance of the individual rings true for us. As we consider what it means to claim God's power in order to live heroically, a question that we might keep before us is, "What difference will it make that I did not die at birth?"

What does it mean to be a hero? When have you seen someone acting heroically or felt that you yourself did something heroic? What made the action heroic? Develop a group definition for the word *hero*. Display the definition in your classroom, and revisit it at the end of each session to see if you want to add to or change the wording.

The word *hero* came into the English language from the Latin language, which had appropriated it from a Greek word meaning demi-god. The word originally came from a Greek root meaning to watch over or to protect. In Greek mythology heroes were individuals—often said to have been born of one mortal and one divine parent—who were endowed with great courage and strength and who were celebrated for their bold exploits.

*The American Heritage Dictionary of the English Language* defines *hero* as "a person noted for feats of courage or nobility of purpose, especially one who has risked or sacrificed his or her life." A second definition is "a person noted for special achievement in a particular field."

The persons we tend to celebrate as modern-day heroes more often fit the second definition. We look up to sports notables, entertainment celebrities, and political figures; and we measure their importance by their popularity in the media and by the economic rewards they enjoy.

Whether we are thinking of heroes in terms of the first or second definition, we

> Make a list of well-known persons that you admire and/or consider to be heroes.

tend to see them as somehow larger than life, persons who, like the Greek heroes of legend, are not quite like us. We might yearn for the fame of the hero, but most of us doubt that we will ever be called heroes.

Thomas Carlyle, a nineteenth-century Scottish philosopher, studied the role of the hero in Western thought and literature. He defined the hero as one who works for change in the midst of adversity. To Carlyle, the hero endures without complaining. At the same time, fueled by some inner light or inspiration, the hero seeks to transform the present into something better. Mere resistance to adversity is not heroism as Carlyle defines it. The hero acts out of an inspired truth that sees beyond the adversity and that transforms both the self and the observer. The hero is what any of us could become if we had that inspired truth or inner light.

I don't know whether my grandmother on my father's side ever read any of Carlyle's work, but I think her life was an example of Carlyle's style of hero. Her pioneering family moved from Iowa to the Dakota Territory when she was only three years old. Growing up on the prairie, she had limited educational opportunities. Her elementary schooling would have been in one-room rural schools, and she may have attended high school in a small prairie town. She was an avid reader and self-educator, and she managed to get advanced schooling at the University of Dakota—an unusual accomplishment for a woman in the late 1800s.

She became a schoolteacher and was teaching in a small Iowa town when she met my grandfather, a local farmer. Marriage, in her day, meant giving up a teaching career; and so she settled into the role of farm wife. Eventually, she became the mother of nine children, eight of whom survived infancy. She never lost her passion for education, and her fondest wish was that her children would have opportunities for higher education. She persuaded her husband to move to Brookings County, South Dakota, in 1910 because she knew that a land-grant college had been established there some twenty years earlier. She wanted her children to attend that school.

Her three oldest sons were by that time beyond the normal age for college entrance and did not respond to her inspiration. She was sorely disappointed when the fourth, my father, dropped out of high school during his freshman year. His next younger brother completed high school but did not see the need for further education. Nothing seemed to be coming of my grandmother's hopes and dreams. I suspect she was not supported in them by my grandfather, who had not gone beyond secondary education himself.

And then tragedy struck. She developed colon cancer. An operation bought her two years, though not comfortable ones. During those two years, she read through the Bible twice. My aunt, who was fifteen when my grandmother died, told me fifty-six years later, "She taught me so much about what to expect of life that to this day I still recall our discussions." That aunt received her degree from South Dakota State College in 1929. Her two younger brothers followed her.

I wish that my grandmother, who would never have called herself a hero, could have known during her lifetime that three of her children did fulfill her dream. I wish that she could have known that the high-school dropout had five children, all of whom graduated from that school and two of whom earned advanced degrees. She had a hope and a dream that was not fulfilled in her lifetime. But years later, it was fulfilled.

Form teams of two or three. Discuss situations you know about or have experienced in which a positive outcome resulted from someone's enduring a difficult situation while working to make it better.

In this study we will consider heroism, not from the standpoint of the world or of popular culture, but from the standpoint of faith. We will look at some Scriptural examples of persons who practiced personal virtues that, when seen through the lens of faith, resulted in heroic behavior. In so doing, we may discover how God is calling us to heroic living and how God equips us to answer the call. Perhaps Carlyle's conception of an inspired truth or inner light is simply God's invitation to us to participate in God's power to change what *is* to what *might be*.

## Daniel: A Pampered POW

From time to time war stories from earlier eras capture the public imagination. While we anxiously follow news events of current wars, we seem to need the palliatives of time and distance in order to explore the lessons and the drama of war. Films and novels set in World War II interest us in the twenty-first century because we look back upon that era as a heroic time for Americans. Stories from the American Civil War fascinate us for the human drama that was played out in a less than heroic time in our history. While modern technology has vastly changed the face of war, human nature hasn't changed much from biblical times. Just as we learn lessons and gain comfort from studying the hard times of our past, the people of biblical Palestine, during a

What war movies, documentaries, or novels have you seen or read? What lessons for the present can be learned from these resources?

13

time of national tribulation, gained comfort and resolve by being reminded of an earlier conflict in their history.

In the second century B.C., the geographical area known as Palestine had fallen into the hands of Syria, a country that had been formed in the breakup of the empire of Alexander the Great. Under Seleucid rule, classic Greek culture prevailed in Syria; and Antiochus IV Epiphanes was determined to assimilate his Jewish subjects into that culture. He appointed high priests that were not of the high-priestly lineage; plundered Jerusalem, stripping treasures from the temple; forced Jews to violate Mosaic law; murdered orthodox Jews in the sacred area; annulled Jewish feasts; and generally belittled Judaism. He attempted to gain political loyalty by dominating religious views.

**For More Information**

Look at a map of Palestine and the Near East during the Maccabean revolt. Read about Antiochus Epiphanes, the Maccabees, and the Maccabean Revolt in a Bible dictionary.

Some time during Antiochus' reign and the Maccabean revolt that it generated, a pious Jew wrote a book to encourage his suffering fellow-believers. He did not write a political treatise on the current situation, however. He wrote a book about another dark page in Jewish history, the Babylonian captivity that had occurred in 586 B.C., about 400 years before the reign of Antiochus IV Epiphanes. In the stories of that earlier war, his readers could draw inferences for their current situation and could hear a message of hope. The hero of his book was a young prisoner of war named Daniel.

**For More Information**

Look up the Babylonian Exile in a Bible dictionary.

It was a political custom during the time of the setting of Daniel for conquering nations to carry off the brightest and best of their victims to their own lands. By doing so they not only weakened the resistance of the conquered peoples but also gained useful service from their captives.

Some of the captives were trained for posts of importance in the king's court, a practice that seems strange to us. But there was method in such madness. Those were days of volatile political upheaval, and the kings of Asia Minor and the Middle East held tenuous rule. At any moment a coup might be led by a brother, a cousin, or a trusted general of the army. So it made sense to surround themselves with leadership that could not recruit a strong following close at hand. At the same time, the foreign captives provided a link to their homelands. The kings thus sought to maintain their power through political patronage.

So it was, according to the writer, that Daniel, an Israelite captive, was one of a group of young men chosen to be trained in the language, literature, and customs of his Babylonian captors. The training period was to last three years, and at the end of that time Daniel could expect to be given an office of honor in the king's court. As POW treatment goes, Daniel had a good deal. But there was one hitch.

As favored prisoners, the trainees were to be given royal treatment, including a daily portion of the royal rations of food

Daniel was a captive. Since he had no choice about being in a foreign land, wouldn't it be understandable and pardonable if he ate what he was given? What was the issue here?

and wine. Daniel, a devout practitioner of the Jewish religion, recognized that he could not eat what was offered without breaking Jewish dietary laws.

At some risk to himself, Daniel approached the palace master, apparently the person in charge of the training program, and requested a vegetarian diet and water for himself and three friends. That dignitary refused, saying that he was afraid of the king's wrath if it should be discovered that the some of the captives had not been fed the rations the king had ordered, especially if, under their requested diet, their health and level of fitness were to be found not to match that of their fellow prisoners. Nice try, Daniel.

So Daniel had made the effort to change the situation and had failed. A lesser person might have given up at this point but not Daniel. His next tactic was to make a deal with their personal guard. Let them try the requested diet for ten days and then compare their appearance to that of the other prisoners. The guard agreed, and the test had a positive outcome. Daniel and his companions were then allowed to eat vegetables and drink only water for the rest of the training period.

The point was not that Daniel knew that a vegetarian diet would be healthier. He didn't have the benefit of our scientific views on nutrition. No, Daniel was simply determined to follow the commands of his faith, and he trusted that the God of his faith would take care of him. Daniel's was not the kind of belief that was compromised at the first sign of danger, and the practices of his faith were important to him. Perhaps in the large view of things what those young Israelites ate and drank was a small matter, but to them it was a symbol of a standard of life they were determined to cling to in a foreign land and in enemy territory. Eating became an act of devotion that gave them hope and comfort and preserved their religious identity.

## Jesse Miller

Jesse Miller, like Daniel, was a prisoner of war, but his situation could not have been more different. In December of 1941, at the age of 20, he was stationed at Clark Air Field in the Philippines, where he worked as a mechanic. Ten hours after the attack on Pearl Harbor, the Japanese bombed his base and invaded the island. The group of soldiers Miller was with eluded the Japanese in the jungle for three months. Eventually they were captured and were forced to join thousands of other U. S. prisoners of war on what would later be called the Bataan Death March. Before the march, Japanese soldiers confiscated all of the prisoners' property, including Jesse's Bible. Jesse lost only the physical counterpart of that book. His real Bible was in his head, for he had long since memorized long passages of the words inside the book that was taken away. For the next few years, he would find strength in those words,

Though Jesse saw many of his comrades die on the march, he managed to survive and was eventually transferred to one of the cargo boats called "hell ships," which was headed for Japan. In Japan, he was forced to work in coalmines to aid the war effort. The work was bone crushing, and he was often in poor health. Still, he clung to his faith.

In his autobiography, he recounts a time in the coalmines when one of his buddies heard him quietly singing hymns in the place many considered hell on Earth. "Miller, you are crazy," the man told him. "The craziest creature I ever met."

Jesse Miller called his autobiography *Prisoner of Hope*. "I was a Prisoner of Hope—not a prisoner of despair, or of ... deep trial and daily pain and injustice," he wrote. "My great daily expectation was that of deliverance in the midst of all things being against me.

"As a prisoner of war, there was no physical fortress to which I could return. All safety and security was cut off from me. No human association or powerful government, no plan of escape could provide the security I needed. But there was always my fortress, my God, to whom I returned."[2]

Just as the disciplines of a devotional life sustained the Daniel of Jesse Miller's Bible, the disciplines of Scripture recitation, hymn singing, and prayer helped Jesse survive some of the most horrible situations imaginable. After the war he spent a long lifetime in ministry to servicemen overseas and in the United States. Jesse Miller didn't

> Who are the Jesse Millers in your congregation? Talk about persons whose loyalty to a devotional life has set an example for you. Do you consider such persons heroes? Why or why not?

set out to be a hero. He simply kept the faith. He died at the age of 80 in 2001.

## Daniel: A Besieged Political Leader

Fast-forward several years in Daniel's life. He had distinguished himself as a political leader in the foreign court and was now being considered by the current king, Darius, for appointment as grand vizier. Darius, having recently ascended to the throne, had divided the country into political divisions called satrapies, each having a ruler called a satrap. The satraps reported to three presidents, one of whom was Daniel. Daniel had so impressed Darius that he planned to appoint him over the entire kingdom, second only to the king himself. Had such power gone to Daniel's head? Apparently not. His political antagonists (can there be politics without political antagonists?), seeking to discredit him in the king's eyes, "could find no grounds for complaint or any corruption … in him" (Daniel 6:4).

> Read the sixth chapter of Daniel. What challenges you or makes you want to know more?

Not only had Daniel been faithful in all things having to do with his occupation, he had also continued to practice a life of devotion to his God. Three times a day, every day of his life, he went to his own chambers for private prayer. There, in a rooftop room with windows opening in the direction of Jerusalem, Daniel knelt devoutly in praise.

> What is a symbolic homeland for you? How do you stay centered?

Facing toward Jerusalem was historically a symbolic act for Jews, who were enjoined to turn toward their homeland for prayer when they were in foreign lands and to turn toward Jerusalem in their own land, just as Muslims turn to Mecca for prayer to this day. The act was a centering one that helped keep the things near at hand in proper perspective.

A conspiracy was formed against Daniel by the other presidents and the satraps, who were jealous of his power. Because they could find nothing in his political life with which to charge him, their only hope was to attack his personal religious practices. But they had to do so carefully, because he was, after all, the king's closest advisor.

The plan they came up with was both brilliant and devious. Appealing to the king's ego, they suggested that Darius establish a thirty-day period during which no one in the kingdom could pray to anyone, divine or human, except the king. Darius, flattered by the proposition, signed it into law, with the stipulation that transgressors would be thrown into a den of lions.

Here was the real test of Daniel's devotion, and his response was as predictable as his enemies knew it would be In Daniel's understanding, the power of God was stronger than the power of the king. Daniel did not miss a single prayer period.

### Law of the Medes and the Persians

At the time of the setting of the Book of Daniel, Media and Persia were separate nations, though they later were joined under one king, Cyrus II. The Medes and the Persians may have been known to follow a common set of laws. Medes, especially, were known for the irrevocable character of their laws, which even a king could not alter without the consent of his government.

When Daniel's enemies informed the king (as they had planned to do all along), Darius saw at once that he had been tricked at Daniel's expense. He was frantic to save his favored servant and struggled with the problem until sunset (presumably several hours). We might wonder why he didn't just rescind his earlier edict. Even though he was the king, his hands were tied by the law of the Medes and the Persians, a legal code that dictated that his earlier injunction must be carried out.

It is interesting that Daniel's devotion to God and his practices

Read aloud verses Daniel 6:26-27.

of faith had not escaped the notice of the king, whose last words to Daniel before sealing him in with the royal menagerie were "May your God, *whom you faithfully serve,* deliver you" (6:16, italics added). And after a sleepless night of worry, the king's first words, upon approaching the lion's den were, "O Daniel, servant of the living God, has your God *whom you faithfully serve* been able to deliver you from the lions?" (6:20, italics added). The lesson the writer of Daniel was seeking to convey is that personal acts of devotion, while they are between us and God, are also a witness to those around us, and they can sway even kings.

How is Daniel a hero? What characteristics make him a hero? What specific heroic actions does he perform? What are the consequences of his heroism?

Daniel was not eaten by the lions, and the story ended victoriously. The king seemed to have what we would call a conversion experience and praised Daniel's God throughout his kingdom.

Daniel claimed God's power for dealing with hard times by fueling himself with consistent prayer and the following of dietary laws. What spiritual disciplines help you claim God's power?

Daniel made a difference in this story, not because he sought to be a hero, but because he kept his focus on God and because he claimed God's power in his life by continuing to practice devotion to God as he went about the everyday business that his office involved. As Christians, we are not called to seek heroic stature; we are called to be faithful in our everyday lives. We may not have influence on a king, but others do watch our actions.

A father and his teenage son were discussing sports figures and the fact that certain players commanded a higher yearly salary than either father or son would see in their lifetime. The father, however, did not share his son's awe for the "heroes" in question. "Son," he advised, "if you want to learn about real heroes, get the newspaper and read the obituaries section. There you will read about real folks who faced all kinds of difficulties in life but who went on about their business, raised their children, and generally left the world better than they found it. Take your lessons from them." We might take our lessons from Daniel.

## Closing Moments

Consider again the definition for *hero* that you created at the beginning of this session. After studying Chapters 1 and 6 in the Book of Daniel, what, if anything, would you add to the definition? Spend some time rewording the definition, and post your new definition for the next session.

Use the prayer at the end of "Opening Moments" (page 9). Find the hymn "God of Love and God of Power" or the hymn "God of Grace and God of Glory" in your church hymnal, and end your time together by singing either hymn.

---

[1]From "The Decline of Heroes," by Arthur M. Schlesinger, in *Adventures of the Mind*, edited by Richard Thruelsen and John Kobler. New York: Vintage Books, 1960.
[2]Reported in "A Colorado Life: Spreading Peace Through Grace," by Jim Sheeler, in the *Denver Post*, March 25, 2001.

## Intergenerational Activity

Plan and participate in a group worship activity using the story of Daniel. Form intergenerational teams to write prayers, choose hymns, and read Scripture. Pay particular attention to incorporating the ideas of children and youth. Offer the worship activity as the closing activity for an intergenerational group like VBS.

# Esther:
# Heroism as Moral Choice

**Focus:** The story of Esther emphasizes heroism as a calling to make right choices in current circumstances. Esther was called to be loyal to the very community that had equipped her to respond to such a calling.

---

**Opening Moments**

Read 1 Corinthians 16:13-14, displayed either on a large sheet of posterboard or on a chalkboard. As you did in Session 1, use this verse as a group greeting. Quickly divide into five clusters (individuals, pairs, or small groups, depending on your numbers) for the reading. Each cluster in turn is to stand and read with conviction one of the phrases beginning with a verb. Each cluster should remain standing until the reading ends.

*"Keep alert, stand firm in your faith, be courageous, be strong. Let all that you do be done in love." (1 Corinthians 16:13-14)*

Pray the following prayer:
Lord of our lives, in a culture where hero worship is so often based on false standards of economics, entertainment, and fame, help us to remember that your ways are not our ways. Keep us mindful that you call the most unlikely people to be heroes in a hurting and needy world. Help us to be alert to situations in our daily lives that call us to choose heroic action over inaction. Help us to draw courage from the community of faith in order that we may be the persons you call us to be in our own time and place. These things we ask in Jesus' name. Amen.

---

## A Holiday Based on a Story of Heroism

Of all Jewish festivals, the most joyful is Purim, held on the fourteenth and fifteenth of Adar, the twelfth month of the Jewish year (around the end of February). Purim has become a celebration of the survival of the Jews in the face of all threats to existence. The holiday is based on a story of perfidy and heroism set in the time of the height of the Persian Empire, about five hundred years before the Christian era. During this time, pockets of Jews lived throughout the Persian Empire (which extended from India to Ethiopia and included Palestine) because of an earlier deportation that had been carried out by Palestine's conquerors around 597 B.C. The story is told in the Book of Esther.

In the beginning of the story, Ahasueras, the Persian king, became angry with his queen, Vashti, because of her refusal to be paraded in front of his male guests, political and military leaders from around the empire, at a banquet. Her refusal to be shown off as the king's trophy wife put the king in a bad light. The king's counselors advised that such rebelliousness could not be permitted. It would set a bad example for wives throughout the

The reasons for Vashti's refusal are not given in the story. What might they have been? Is Vashti a hero? Why or why not?

kingdom, who might get the idea that they too could challenge their husbands' demands. Ahasueras agreed to depose the queen and to hold a contest to determine her successor (only beautiful young virgins need apply). Candidates from around the empire were invited to live in the king's harem for a year while they were groomed to perfection. Then each had one night to delight the king. The new queen would be the woman who pleased him most.

## Esther, the Beauty Queen

Among the contestants for the role of replacement queen was Esther, a young Jewish orphan who had been raised by her older cousin Mordecai, a minor official in the Persian court. Perhaps through his connections at court, Mordecai had been able to push his ward forward. The story does not suggest that she went unwillingly. Before Esther entered the harem, Mordecai cautioned her to keep her ethnic identity a secret.

Esther quickly charmed Hegai, the official in charge of the harem, and received preferential treatment (seven maids from the palace, the best place in the harem) during her year of preparation. When her turn came to go to Ahasuerus, she relied on Hegai's judgment as to what would please the king. As a result, we learn that "the king loved Esther more than all the other women; of all the virgins she won his favor and devotion, so that he set the royal crown on her head and made her queen instead of Vashti" (2:17).

So far we have seen a side of Esther that is not necessarily admirable from a Christian point of view. Her uncle's influence has placed her in this questionable beauty contest, and she has used her feminine wiles to curry the favor of the official who can be of the most help to her in beating out the other candidates. She hardly

> What traits of character would you assign to Esther at this point in the story? Are these marks of a hero? Why or why not?

seems to possess the characteristics of a hero. Yet any careful reading of the Old and New Testaments reveals that biblical heroes were not always models of moral perfection. Jacob, the patriarch who preserved Abraham's lineage, stole the family inheritance from his brother Esau and then fled rather than face Esau's wrath. King David, who united the nations of Judah and Israel under his rule, committed adultery with the wife of one of his generals and then issued orders that effectively led to the man's death. The closest followers of Jesus, who later became leaders of the church, forsook their leader and fled when he was arrested by Roman soldiers. Esther seems no better and no worse than several other biblical headliners.

Throughout the biblical record, God calls people who are less than perfect—ordinary people like you and me—to become the instruments through which God acts. All persons who respond to God's call to be God's advocates in the midst of his or her everyday life are also called to serve. What can we learn from these heroes of Scripture?

> What other examples can you name of biblical heroes who were less-than-perfect role models?

For one thing, we do not have to be perfect before we can act on God's behalf. God does not wait for us to develop heroic stature. Living heroically only requires that we be faithful. As we respond to God in faith, we are called to be God's persons in our own place and time to do the work that God has for us to do.

## Haman's Plot

All the elements were set in place for the unfolding of Esther's story. Mordecai made an enemy in the court, a man named Haman who had risen to the post of grand vizier. By refusing to bow down to Haman, Mordecai incited Haman's wrath, but Haman was a particularly vengeful villain. He knew that Mordecai was a Jew; and he decided to take revenge, not just on Haman, but also on the entire Jewish population of the empire. He cast lots to decide when his revenge would be accomplished. Then, after convincing Ahasuerus that "a certain people" scattered around the kingdom adhered to a different set of laws than the king's laws and were a dangerous element, Haman obtained the king's permission to see that these people were destroyed. Haman used the king's signet ring to post a royal decree throughout the kingdom ordering the destruction of the Jews and the plundering of their property on the thirteenth of Adar.

### Jews of the Diaspora (Dispersion)

During the Babylonian Exile, Jews who were carried off to foreign lands were determined not to forget their heritage and their religion. In order not to be assimilated into the cultures of their captivity, they clung to the laws and customs of Jewish life., passing them on to each new generation. They were determined not to intermarry with their captors and generally lived together in ethnic sections of towns and provinces.

Examining the story from our vantage point, we can understand that Haman's decree pandered to the fear of ethnic differences. His behavior toward the Jews in this story is not unlike anti-Semitic activity that has occurred in post-biblical times.

## For Such a Time as This

When Mordecai learned what Haman had done, he sent a message to Queen Esther through one of her servants, charging her to plead the cause of the Jews with the king. Esther replied that for fear of death she could not appear before the king without being bidden and that the king had not called on her for a month. Mordecai's return message cut to the chase: "Do not think that in the king's palace you will escape any more than all the other Jews. For if you keep silence at such a time as this, relief and deliverance will rise for the Jews from another quarter, but you and your father's family will perish" (4:13-14).

J. Perry Parker, a retired Air Force chaplain, entered the military at an early age. He recalls that on the day that he left for the Navy at eighteen, his mother had only one piece of advice for him: "Son, remember who you are." Those words have stayed with him for a lifetime. Her advice was different from the normal cautionary "Don't be a hero." In fact, Mrs. Parker was suggesting an opposite approach. What her words meant, her son says, was "You come from honorable people who have always tried to make right choices and to conduct themselves with dignity and with compassion toward others." This mother put her son in touch with his heritage and trusted that, being thus grounded, he would not disappoint her.

In the biblical story, Mordecai, Esther's adoptive father, reminded her of such grounding. In essence, his message was "Woman, remember who you are." When Mordecai said that deliverance for the Jews would rise from some other quarter if Esther did not act, his words were a reminder that the Jews had always been a chosen people and that the God of Esther's ancestors—the God of Abraham, Isaac, Jacob, Moses, and David—would not forsake the Jews in Esther's time. Nevertheless, Esther had a unique opportunity to be God's instrument, and loyalty to her people demanded that she act. Mordecai replied, "Who knows? Perhaps you have come to royal dignity for just such a time as this" (4:14).

Some translations use the word *kingdom* in place of the words *royal dignity,* and I have always liked that wording. Although Mordecai is referring to the royal court of the Persian Empire, there are times when each of us is called to God's kingdom for just such a time as our circumstances dictate. The adage "If not now, when? If not me, who?" applies to every individual. We sometimes face situations in which we know that other persons are better qualified to deal with the realities at hand, but we cannot always wait for those persons to appear. God's admonition to us may be "You are the person in this time and in this place to deal with this predicament." We are not called to seek heroism; we are called to faithful obedience to God in the everyday circumstances of our lives, an obedience that points to the potential for true heroic action. We are called to be God's person in our place and time.

> What situations have you had to deal with in spite of feeling unqualified or unprepared? What was the result of your action or of your failure to act?

## If I Perish, I Perish

In the story, Esther rose to the challenge and agreed to do the right thing regardless of her fear. "I will go to the king, though it is against the law; and if I perish, I perish" (4:16). Esther chose to be involved and to let the chips fall where they may; and in so doing, she chose the heroic course.

Facing hard times does not guarantee that one will act heroically. Heroism is accomplished through God's grace, but the role is by no means a passive one. We are not puppets in the hands of a divine Creator. God may call us to heroic action, but, as is the case with Esther, how we answer is our choice. We can always choose to say no.

In the film *Mr. Holland's Last Opus,* the main character, a high school music teacher, works in a school where the female principal does not always agree with his teaching methods. Nevertheless, this principal is fair-minded and is always willing to be convinced that Mr. Holland knows what he is doing. Eventually the principal retires and is replaced by a younger man. Shortly thereafter, the new principal announces to Mr. Holland that the school board, in response to a budget crisis, has decided to eliminate the school's music program. Mr. Holland questions whether the principal has defended the music program to the board, saying that the principal's predecessor would have done so. The principal says that the decision was ironclad and that his predecessor would have been foolish to raise any objections. He insists that she would have lost the battle. Mr. Holland replies, "But she would have fought it."

Life-and-death situations do not often present themselves to most of us, yet I can think of a time in my own experience that called for Esther's kind of resolve.

> Are there some battles that are worth the fight even though the odds are against winning? How can we be heroic even when losing?

In 1967 my husband joined the army voluntarily to train for service as a helicopter pilot. During his year of training prior to being shipped to Vietnam, I discovered that I was pregnant with our first child (definitely not something for which we had planned). Although family furloughs had been a practice of earlier wars, the military's attitude was different in this conflict. In my eighth month of pregnancy, I found myself standing on a tarmac bidding good-bye to my husband, not knowing whether I would see him again. How vividly I can recall his kissing me and telling me to take care of our unborn child, then walking stiff-backed to the plane and never looking back. Tearing himself away from me took tremendous courage on his part. And I was thinking, *If he perishes, he perishes; and I will raise this child.* I watched until the plane became a dot in the sky and disappeared.

## Reinforcement From the Community

After making her resolve, Esther sought the support of her faith community. "Go, gather all the Jews to be found in Susa," she says to Mordecai, "and neither eat nor drink for three days, night or day. I and my maids will also fast as

> Share personal experiences or situations that you know about that have called for heroic resolve.

29

you do" (4:16). Fasting was a religious practice of the Jewish community and was accompanied by prayer. Esther asked for the prayers of her people to sustain her in her undertaking.

British author J.R.R. Tolkien, writing during World War II, created a fantasy world called Middle Earth as the setting for his *Lord of the Rings* trilogy (made into three Hollywood blockbuster movies in recent years). In *Lord of the Rings,* Tolkien raises the question of what makes a person a hero. The work supplies a simple answer: A hero is not necessarily the person with the biggest sword; rather, a hero is the person with the biggest heart who is willing to sacrifice for others. The true heroes of Tolkien's story are Frodo Baggins and Sam Gamgee, members of a peace-loving race of little people called hobbits. While great and powerful forces of good and evil are fighting a war to determine the entire future of Middle Earth, the outcome that saves their world is determined by a journey made by these two very ordinary individuals. What makes them heroic is their devotion to the cause of returning the ring of power to the place where it originated, where no one can use it for evil purposes. They are supported in their task by the fellowship of the ring, a close-knit group of friends that includes two other hobbits, two humans, a wizard, an elf, and a dwarf. All the members of this unlikely band are dedicated to the cause of helping Frodo, the ring bearer, succeed. Just as Esther relied on her faith community to sustain her, the comradeship and backing of this close-knit community give Frodo and Sam encouragement for the journey.

Likewise, as Christians we do not face our circumstances in isolation. The support and resources of the Christian community are always available to us when we "remember who we are." Our church was a mainstay to our family throughout our Vietnam experience. Besides holding us up daily in prayer, they helped pay for the plane tickets that carried me and our three-month-old son to Hawaii so that my

If you have read Tolkien's trilogy or seen one, two, or all three of the *Lord of the Rings* motion pictures, discuss the struggles, failures, and triumphs of the major characters.

husband could see his child for the first time during a week's respite from the war. The support of our faith community helped us do what we had to do during a difficult time in our lives.

## "Let's Roll!"

Among the many heroic stories that came out of the tragic events of September 11, 2001, was that of United Airlines flight 93, which crashed in rural Pennsylvania after the passengers attempted to regain control of the hijacked plane. It wasn't those people's job to fight terrorists. They simply did what they had to do in an attempt to foil evil intentions. They were God's persons in a place and time that they could never have anticipated. One of those passengers was Todd Beamer, a 32-year-old Oracle software account manager from Cranbury, New Jersey, who gave the world the catch phrase "Let's roll!" as a word of triumphant defiance in the face of evil.

Before he participated in the heroic event that led to his death, Todd Beamer made a telephone call to the GTE Customer Center in Oakbrook, Illinois, a suburb of Chicago. He wanted to report the hijacking, and he needed to talk to someone. The Airfone operator at Station 15 turned his call over to her supervisor, Lisa Jefferson, who talked calmly with Beamer and was able to comfort him in his final minutes. Just as Esther asked the community of faith to fast and pray on her behalf, Todd Beamer asked Lisa Jefferson to recite the Lord's Prayer with him, and she did. Then she stayed on the line with him until he said it was time to go. She later told a Sentinel National correspondent that she was glad she was able to be there for Todd Beamer, but she didn't think anyone would ever want to be in that situation. She related feeling that God's role for her was to answer that call and to remain calm. Lisa Jefferson's faith in God and her seventeen years of experience as an Airfone operator had prepared her to deal with an event that she too could never have anticipated. She was God's person in that place on that particular day; and the support of her own faith community had equipped her for that role.

In the biblical story, Esther went to the inner court with mixed emotions of courage and fear. There she stood and bravely waited to see if the king would offer her his royal scepter, thus granting her an audience. The penalty for approaching the king without being bidden was death, a consequence that sounds unnecessarily harsh. Such a law made sense for politically perilous times, however, serving as a means of protecting the king from assassins. Ahasueras, seeing his queen, held out the scepter to her and invited her into his presence.

> How might your participation in this group and in the faith community of which it is a part be equipping you for heroic action? What characteristics of the community might prepare you to deal with unanticipated crises? Whom would you call on if you needed the kind of support that Esther and Todd Beamer needed?

Esther once again used her feminine guile to influence the king, this time not to win a crown but to save her people from annihilation. Through a subsequent series of events that Esther orchestrated, she managed to get rid of Mordecai's enemy, Haman; and she plead for the lives of her people, the Jews.

Ahasuerus had been unaware of the identity of the "certain people" that Haman's decree, sent under the king's seal, would cause to be destroyed. The king was sympathetic and told Esther and Mordecai that they could send out any new decree that they wished but that the old decree, according to the law of the Medes and the Persians (see page 19), could not be revoked.

> Form teams of two or three. Discuss: What characteristics made her a hero? What specific heroic actions did she perform? What are the consequences of her heroism? In light of what you know about such anti-Semitic events as the Spanish Inquisition, the Holocaust, and other pogroms against the Jews throughout history, what meaning do you think the Festival of Purim can have for Jews today? Share small-group answers in the total group.

Mordecai sent out a new decree that enabled the Jews to defend themselves against any who attacked them on the thirteenth of Adar.

Throughout the kingdom on the thirteenth of Adar, the Jews won the day. The next two days were named as days of celebration. Purim remains a time of celebration for Jews today. Purim is the Persian word for lots, and the name of the festival derives from Haman's having cast lots to choose the day of the Jews' destruction in Persia.

**Closing Moments**

Consider again the definition for hero that you created in the previous session. After considering the story of Esther, what, if anything, would you add to the definition? Spend some time rewording the definition, and post your new definition for the next session.

Pray again the prayer at the end of "Opening Moments" (page 23). Find the hymn "Here I Am, Lord" or the hymn "Whom Shall I Send?" in your church hymnbook, and end your time together by singing either hymn.

## For an Extended Session
## or an Intergenerational Activity

Invite a Jewish rabbi to attend your session. Ask him or her to be prepared to explain how Purim is celebrated in your locality and what Purim means to local Jewish congregations.

# Four Friends:
# Tenacious Compassion

**Focus:** Four friends who brought a paralyzed man to Jesus for healing were members of a compassionate community. Their determination to help their friend in spite of obstacles was fueled by their faith in Jesus as a healer.

### Opening Moments

Read the words of 1 Corinthians 16:13-14 displayed either on a large sheet of posterboard or on a chalkboard. As you did in previous sessions, use this verse as a group greeting. Quickly divide into five clusters (individuals, pairs, or small groups, depending on your numbers) for the reading. Each cluster in turn is to stand and read with conviction one of the phrases beginning with a verb. Each cluster should remain standing until the reading ends.

*"Keep alert, stand firm in your faith, be courageous, be strong. Let all that you do be done in love." (1 Corinthians 16:13-14)*

Pray the following prayer:
Gracious and loving Father, as we strive to live heroically for you, let our motives be fueled by compassion. Help us to confront the needs of a hurting world and not look away. Grant us determination and strength that we may not falter in our attempts to deal with suffering in its many forms and in our efforts to foster healing. As we minister to our neighbors' needs, help us not grow weary in well doing. Help us to understand that any ministry we undertake is a partnership with you and that you will be with us regardless of obstacles to be overcome. Help us to deal with obstacles with ingenuity and determination borne by our faith and by the support of our faith community. These things we ask in Jesus' name. Amen.

## A Man With Friends

Perhaps they had only heard accounts of Jesus' healing ministry. Or maybe some of their numbers had been in the synagogue when Jesus cured a man with an unclean spirit. Some of them

Read Mark 2:1-4. What strikes you as interesting or unusual about this story? What challenges you or makes you curious?

could have been in the crowds in any of the Galilean towns where Jesus proclaimed his message and healed the sick. Or perhaps they had run into the man who no longer suffered from leprosy after touching Jesus' hand. Whatever the stimulus for their actions, the community around the paralyzed man knew that they had found a way to end their friend's suffering. All they had to do was get him to Jesus.

We do not know how large this compassionate group was. The Gospel accounts refer to them as "some people," and Mark says that four among them—perhaps the stoutest four—carried his pallet.

So here was a man desperately ill yet rich in friends who truly cared for him. He could not walk. He must have been dependent on others for a long time before Jesus spoke words of healing to him. Who had secured his food and had seen that he continued to be fed? Who had helped him bathe? What about times when he had wanted to be outdoors soaking up some sunshine? Had he been included in the social activities of the community? We can surmise that friends who cared enough to want him healed probably had been performing small acts of compassion toward him on a daily basis, in so many little ways

What would it feel like to be totally dependent on others for the daily activities you take for granted? If you suddenly became debilitated, who would be in your support community?

already claiming God's power in the man's behalf. Even in his state of paralysis, he was blessed.

## A Modern-Day Equivalent

My friend Annie joined a church-sponsored group focusing on attitudinal healing, not because she had health problems, but because she was intrigued by the topic and wanted to learn more about it. Word of the group's efforts spread. Among those who came to find out more about what they were doing was a young man who clearly needed a lot of help. He was estranged from his family, possibly because he had a history of drug abuse; and his physical health was poor at best. His kidneys had failed, and his survival depended on his undergoing peritoneal dialysis on a daily basis. His insurance had provided a portable machine so that he could be treated at home; but the treatment, in order to be safely accomplished, required someone to administer it. This man was alone.

Here was a challenge for a Christian community that had said that it was interested in healing. Annie became part of a small group who took on the man's care. This group of friends learned how the dialysis machine worked and the process of sterilization that was necessary to get it ready. They took turns staying with the man when he was undergoing dialysis. Not the most pleasant aspect of their assignment was the need to spend the night on a sofa in the man's shabby apartment so that they would be at hand to help if beeps and buzzes from the machine's monitors indicated that something had happened to interrupt or obstruct the treatment.

The group provided moral support as the young man underwent a kidney transplant and subsequent rejection of the organ. They continued to help with his dialysis for another year before a second transplant was successful. During this time, the young man was able to get other aspects of his life on a more positive footing, no doubt influenced by the compassion of a group who had been strangers before he reached out for help. Annie and her friends had claimed God's power on this man's behalf by exercising the virtue of compassion.

> Could you do what Annie and her friends did? Why or why not? Describe experiences you have had or that you know about that called for unusual compassion and care for someone who was in desperate need. What did the situation require? Was it easy or difficult to be compassionate? Why or why not?

Like Annie's group, the biblical community, through their daily, small acts of compassion, had been able to sustain their friend who could not walk; but now there was promise of a greater degree of help for him than the community could provide. Imagine the excitement his friends must have felt as they anticipated his healing and worked out a plan to help make it a reality. They knew where Jesus was housed in Capernaum. Someone in the group was aware that he had returned from traveling throughout Galilee. How could they get their friend to Jesus? Perhaps it took some trial and error for them to determine that four of them could carry him on his pallet. Perhaps they took turns, in groups of four, transporting him. I like to imagine that their mood was a festive one as they bore their friend toward hope and healing.

## Obstacles to Healing

Yet the day was not to be so easily won. A dismaying scene greeted the group's eyes as they came within sight of the house. We are told that so many people had gathered around Jesus that there was no room for anyone else, not even in front of the door. Well, the friends had done their best. Who would have blamed them for saying, "We tried," and then carrying the paralytic man back to his home?

On a chalkboard, markerboard, or large sheet of paper posted on the wall, make a list of obstacles frequently encountered—both as a church and as individual Christians—in efforts to help others. When no one has anything else to add to the list, have the group divide into groups of three. Let each small group choose one obstacle from the list and come up with as many creative ways as they can think of to get around the obstacle in order to be successful in providing help. Share small-group efforts in the total group.

Our efforts in helping others are not always success stories. All kinds of obstacles, from government regulations to resistance to being helped by those who need help most, can make it tempting for us to say, "We tried," and to turn our efforts elsewhere. Paul understood the phenomenon and left enduring words of encouragement: "Let us not grow weary in doing what is right [some translations read *in well doing*], for we will reap at harvest-time, if we do not give up. So then, whenever we have an opportunity, let us work for the good of all, and especially for those of the family of faith" (Galatians 6:9-10).

## Do Heroes Ever Give Up?

What happened next in the biblical story of the paralytic's healing is a tribute to the ingenuity of the man's companions. The paralyzed man certainly knew how to pick his friends.

Homes of the day had flat roofs that were accessed by a set of stairs going up one side of the house so that the family could sleep under the stars in hot weather. The roofs were a composite of branches, twigs, and clay baked in the sun. Mark says that the friends "removed the roof" above Jesus' head in order to lower their friend, still on his pallet, into Jesus' presence.

Imagine the scene: Members of the group mill around their friend, asking one another, "Now what? Does anyone have an idea?" Someone sees the stairs and shouts, "The roof! Can we go through the roof somehow?" A digging tool is needed. Perhaps someone finds a tree branch and trims it to a sharp point. Their digging activity is frenzied. They have come too far to turn back or to give up easily.

Imagine what else the friends might have said. What other suggestions might have been made but rejected in favor of the roof solution? What else might they have usd as a tool?

When have you had to come up with a creative solution in order to solve a problem? Did you have to convince a group that your solution would work? What are the pros and cons of having to work within a group to solve problems?

## Tenacity of Spirit

The biblical friends' tenacity of spirit kept them from giving up. The quality was probably rare then, and it still is; but sometimes we do encounter it.

During the Vietnam Conflict, my husband joined the army for pilot training with the hope of being assigned to a Medivac unit. He was instead assigned to fly Cobra gunships. One of his buddies from flight training was assigned to fly the light observation helicopters (LOH) that were used as scout ships for the Cobras. The scouts flew low reconnaissance missions in advance of the gunships to determine enemy locations and often did so by drawing enemy fire. Pilots ruefully referred to the LOH as the killer egg. My husband's friend survived two LOH crashes before the one that took his life on an occasion when he was flying scout for my husband.

In a letter telling me about his buddy's death, my husband lamented the fact that because his friend was killed in combat, a citation had to be written up recommending the man for a hero's medal for that particular mission. My husband was put off by the hypocrisy of painting a heroic picture of what was in reality a case of being in the wrong place at the right time. Knowing that my husband was grieving his friend's loss, I worded my response carefully, suggesting that his buddy was indeed a hero deserving of the medal, not because he was killed on that occasion, but because he had returned to flying LOH missions after being shot down not once but twice. I pointed out that it was the tenacity of his spirit that made him a hero. In the next letter I received, my husband thanked me for my letter and said that only after reading it was he able to shed tears for his friend.

## A Modern Superhero

Tenacity of spirit has sustained a modern-day paralytic and is bringing about unprecedented progress toward his healing. Actor Christopher Reeve, best known for his starring role in four *Superman* movies, was thrown from a horse during a riding competition on May 27, 1995. Landing on his head, he suffered spinal cord injuries that left him paralyzed below the neck. Medical experts predicted that he would never again be able to feel or move below his shoulders or to breathe on his own without the assistance of a ventilator. For the first few years of his treatment, their predictions proved on target.

Perhaps the medical experts underestimated what a tenacious spirit can do. In the September 23, 2002, issue of *People* magazine, Reeve gave a clue to his approach to life that certainly affects his healing: "The fact is that even if your body doesn't work the way it used to, the heart and the mind and the spirit are not diminished. It's as simple as that." Since his accident, his progress, attitude, and activism have approached legendary status.

With injuries so egregious, who could fault Christopher Reeve for resigning himself to the life that the experts had predicted for him? He admitted to a BBC interviewer that the temptation to feel sorry for himself is always with him but that the way out for him is to think of something that needs doing. He has helped raise millions of dollars for research and has established the Christopher Reeve Paralysis Foundation to do spinal injury research. While confined to his wheelchair, he has been a vocal advocate for a number of medical crusades and has directed and starred in TV productions.

Given Christopher Reeve's hardships, his acting, directing, and advocacy activities are heroic achievements. Considering the extent of his injuries, he has shown remarkable physical restoration. His tenacity of spirit and a consistent regimen of exercise and care have been components of his progress. Some five years after his accident, he began to regain both sensation and movement. By early 2003, he could distinguish between a pinprick and a

If possible, rent a video of the first *Superman* movie and a video of the 1998 made-for-television remake of *Rear Window,* which starred Christopher Reeve; or buy copies online from Amazon.com. View clips from each movie. Compare and contrast the heroism of the two main characters. With which character is it easier to identify? Why?

For an extended session, plan a dinner at someone's home and watch both movies in their entirety. How does seeing each movie affect your feelings as you view the other? What character traits do you admire in each of the protagonists? What character traits do you not admire? In your opinion, who is the greater hero?

light touch over most of his body; could move his right wrist, the fingers of his left hand, and his feet; and could breathe without the help of the ventilator for as long as ninety minutes at a time. Prior to his experience, even the most optimistic experts had thought that such recovery from spinal cord injury was possible only within the first two years. Dr. John McDonald, medical director of the Spinal Cord Injury Program at Washington University School of Medicine in St. Louis, Missouri, says, "No one who has suffered an injury as severe as Chris's, and failed to have any initial recovery, has regained the amount of motor and sensory function he has—not even close."[1]

Healing for Christopher Reeve has been slow, and every improvement has been hard won; but he does not give up the hope of someday being able to walk again. He credits help from his family, his friends, and many dedicated physicians and therapists for the progress he has made. In Christopher Reeve's view, his wife, Dana, is the real hero. He says, "[She] never for a minute looked away or pulled back or doubted."[2]

Form teams of two or three. Discuss: Is Christopher Reeve a hero? What characteristics make him a hero? What specific heroic actions has he performed? If he never walks again, will he be any less a hero? Why or why not? In what ways is his wife Dana a hero? In what ways are the physicians and therapists heroes? What connections do you see between Christopher Reeve's situation and the healing of the paralytic in Mark 2? Describe situations you have experienced or know about where ordinary people who do not have Christopher Reeve's resources have displayed unusual tenacity of spirit in the face of difficulties. Share small-group answers in the total group.

Christopher Reeve knows that the care and expertise of his medical team will play a large part in his accomplishments should he walk again. Likewise, the friends of the paralytic in Mark's story had complete confidence in Jesus' ability to restore their friend's mobility, and they were willing to go to such extreme measures as to tear up a roof to get that kind of help for him.

## Healing and Wholeness

Jesus' first words to the paralytic did not address the physical malady the man suffered. Rather, Jesus said to him, "Son, your sins are forgiven" (2:5). While this pronouncement may seem to us to be unrelated to the man's most critical need, it was not beside the point in Jesus' day. The popular belief of the time

Read Mark 2:5, 11-12. What thoughts or feelings do you have about Jesus' initial response to the man who was paralyzed?

was that any kind of sickness or debility was punishment for sin. Thus those who suffered were thought to have brought on their own misery by their sinful actions. Forgiveness of the sin would seem necessary in order to open the door for physical healing, which Jesus promptly offered the man.

Consider this chronology of events from the sick man's point of view. He had a debilitating condition that he probably believed was his own fault. He may have blamed his condition on something that he had done or had failed to do earlier in his life. It is even possible that feelings of guilt about something that he had

What connections do you see between mental health and physical health? Has your state of mind ever affected how you were feeling physically?

done or left undone had affected his physical well being. If Jesus had only restored the man's ability to walk, guilt over what might have caused his paralysis would still remain with him and could affect his future physical condition. Jesus recognized the need for complete healing. He gave the man not just restored mobility but wholeness of mind and body.

In light of the beliefs of the day, the compassion of the man's friends seems even more admirable. They loved their friend no matter what he may have done to deserve his condition, and their greatest desire for him was that he be well. Their optimism and their complete confidence in Jesus as a healer must have given the man great encouragement even before he was healed. Jesus was touched by their devotion, and Mark says that Jesus' response to the paralytic was a direct result of his seeing the friends' demonstration of faith. Compassion, tenacity of spirit, and trust were the attributes that enabled a group of caring individuals to claim God's power for the healing of their friend.

> Were the paralytic's friends heroes? Why or why not? If so, what characteristics made them heroes? Who are the people who would love you and who would wish for your well being no matter what you did?

## Trust in Jesus' Authority

The friends of the paralyzed man trusted that Jesus could exercise God's healing power on behalf of their friend. Mark 2:12 indicates that those present, including the man's friends, understood that God was the source of Jesus' ability to heal. But not everyone there shared the view that God's power was available in the person of Jesus. Mark records that among the crowd were some scribes, teachers of the law, who were questioning his actions in their hearts. Jesus could sense their disapproval.

> Read Mark 2:6-12. What does this Scripture say to you about trust? about Jesus and the power of God?

The scribes were strict interpreters of the law that had come down from the time of Moses. Their interest was in obeying the law of Moses. For Jesus to say that the man's sins were forgiven was blasphemy to the scribes in that it seemed to claim an authority belonging to God.

Jesus challenged the scribes' right to determine what was holy for other people and to try to limit the conditions under which persons might expect to receive God's mercy. To prove that he spoke for God, Jesus asked the scribes which would be easier, to say that the man's sins had been forgiven or to heal his paralysis.

Jesus' healing of the man ended the debate over Jesus' authority to proclaim God's forgiveness.

## Son of Man

In Mark 2:10, Jesus refers to himself as "the Son of Man," a term that has more than one meaning in the biblical record. In many passages, it means a typical human being. For example, in some translations the prophet Ezekiel is referred to as a son of man. Other translations use the word *mortal*. But in the Book of Daniel, "one like a human being" is presented as one who "was given dominion / and glory and kingship, / that all peoples, nations, and languages / should serve him. / His dominion is an everlasting dominion / that shall not pass away, / and his kingship is one / that shall never be destroyed" (7:13-14). Mark's Gospel uses the term *Son of Man* fourteen times, and all uses are placed in the mouth of Jesus. The Son of Man forgives sins and is lord of the sabbath (2:10, 28), suffers, dies, and rises again (8:31; 9:9, 12, 31; 10:33; 14:41), serves and gives his life as a ransom for many (10:45), and comes in the glory of God with the angels (8:38; 13:26).

## Closing Moments

Consider again the definition for *hero* that you created in previous sessions. After considering the account of the friends of the paralytic, what, if anything, would you add to the definition? Spend some time rewording the definition, and post your new definition for the next session.

Pray again the prayer at the end of "Opening Moments" (page 35). Find the hymn "Through It All" or the hymn "Trust and Obey" in your church hymnbook, and end your time together by singing either hymn.

---

[1]"Whisper of Hope", *People* magazine, September 23, 2002.
[2]BBC NEWS.

## Intergenerational Activity

### Pack Health Kits

As a churchwide project related to this lesson on the healing of the paralytic, children, youth, and adult classes can gather supplies and assemble health kits to be given to refugees, disaster victims, and other persons with limited resources.

Include the following items in each health kit:
• One hand towel
• One wash cloth
• One bath-size bar of soap, any brand, in its original wrapping
• One toothbrush in its original wrapping
• One tube of toothpaste, 5- to 7-oz. size, removed from the box
• One comb, wide-tooth preferred
• One metal nail file, or nail clippers with a file attached, removed from its packaging
• Six bandages, preferably ½" to ¾"

Wrap all items in the towel, and tie it securely with ribbons or yarn. Please note that all items included in the kits must be new. Include all the items listed and do not add items that are not on the list. Though extra gifts are given with the best of intentions, they often make a kit unusable and must be taken out.

Pack completed health kits in sturdy cardboard boxes, and secure with packing tape. Indicate the contents (for example: 25 health kits) on the outside of each box.

The agencies listed on page 47 have warehouses that accept and distribute health kits. Or check with your denominational social-service agency if it is not listed here. Before initiating this project, call or otherwise contact your agency of choice to be sure that it is currently accepting kits.

UMCOR Depot
131 Sager Brown Road
P.O. Box 850
Baldwin, LA 70514-0850
1-800-814-8765
umcor@gbgm-umc.org

American Friends Service Committee
1501 Cherry Street
Philadelphia, PA 19102-7283
215-241-7000
afscinfo@afsc.org

Church World Service
Brethren Service Center Annex
601 Main Street, P.O. Box 188
New Windsor, MD 21776-0188
1-888-297-2767
www.churchworldservice.org

Lutheran World Relief Warehouse
398 E. Richmond Street
South St. Paul, MN 55075
651-457-9009
lwr@lwr.org

# An Unknown Widow:
# Poor in Possessions, Rich in Spirit

**Focus:** Jesus understood that a poor widow's gift to the temple treasury was motivated by a generous heart that enabled her to give in a spirit of selflessness in spite of her hardships.

### Opening Moments

Prepare a worship center. Place colorful fabric on a small table. Place brass candlesticks, a small cross, and an offering plate on the table. Light the candles and dim the room lights.

Read 1 Corinthians 16:13-14, displayed either on a large sheet of posterboard or on a chalkboard, as your group greeting. As you have done in previous sessions, quickly divide into five clusters (individuals, pairs, or small groups, depending on your numbers), and have each cluster in turn stand and read with conviction one of the phrases beginning with a verb. Each cluster should remain standing until the reading ends.

*"Keep alert, stand firm in your faith, be courageous, be strong. Let all that you do be done in love." (1 Corinthians 16:13-14)*

Then pray the following prayer:
Most gracious Father, the source of all our gifts and the ground of our being, fill our hearts with such awareness of your boundless generosity toward us that we are inspired to live lives reflecting your spirit of giving. Help us to be generous. Teach us to give without considering the cost, and grant us joy born of the freedom that comes from not being owned by our possessions. These things we ask in Jesus' name. Amen.

## One Day in the Temple

A feeling of contentment washed over her as she wandered awestruck in the court of the women. Being in the temple always affected her this way. Just to know that she was close to the Holy of Holies, the innermost secret enclosure that was said to house the very presence of God, filled her with a sense of joy that she would have found difficult to describe. And how she loved the beauty of this place. Its gleaming white marble decorated in gold took her breath away. Lovingly her eyes traced gold-leafed relief sculptures of plump grapes clustered on delicate vines. Next she delighted in the jewel tones of multi-colored mosaic floors and beautifully woven tapestries. Truly this building was a fitting monument to the God of her ancestors, the God of Abraham, Isaac, and Jacob, the God whom she worshiped today.

Read the paragraphs in "One Day in the Temple" as a dramatic reading. Toss two pennies into the offering plate at the appropriate time.

"One Day in the Temple" is written in a style called stream of conscious, a literary device that lets the reader inside the mind of a main character as a situation develops. Read Luke 21:1-4. Divide into small groups and create stream-of-consciousness monologues for these other characters in that situation (choose only one if your group is too small to divide): a) a wealthy man who gives a large bag of coins; b) a wealthy man who gives a small bag of coins; c) Jesus; or d) one of the disciples.

As you create your monologues, consider these questions: How does the character feel about being in the temple? What does the character think about the gift he is giving or the gifts he observes being given? For the givers, what does the money represent to them? How did they decide on the amount to give? What does the disciple think of Jesus' reaction to the gifts? What are some of Jesus' concerns as he observes the giving?

Read the monologues to the total group.

She was not permitted to go beyond the women's court to the high altar where the priests presided over animal sacrifices, but from that direction she could hear the voices of the Levites singing Psalms to the accompaniment of reed pipes and other instruments. The tones of their chanting were interlaced with the conversational voices of the crowds around her and the exhortations of teachers in corners of the court debating fine points of the law amid groups of students. She couldn't say why, but the combination of sounds gave her a happy feeling.

She sighed deeply with a grateful heart, glad for this respite from the outside world that was sometimes cruel to her. When her Aaron had died, the settling of their affairs had left her with few resources. In fact, this very day she would have a stretch to find enough provisions for a meal. But she would worry about that later. To reassure herself that they were still there, she reached into a small pocket and fingered the two coins that she had managed to scrape together for this visit.

### Herod's Temple

The temple of Jerusalem, as it existed in Jesus' day, was not an ancient building; in fact, it was still under construction. Herod began rebuilding the temple in 20 B.C., and construction was not completed until 62 A.D. Rebuilding the temple was both a symbol of Herod's prestige and a way of catering to the Jews, who detested his rule. The outer walls of the temple complex surrounded the court of the Gentiles, where even non-Jews could gather and make offerings. Column-lined porches around this court contained the tables of the moneychangers. A stone balustrade and a low flight of steps surrounded the temple precincts, which could be entered by one of three doors opening onto the court of the women. This inner courtyard was not restricted to women but was the point beyond which women were not allowed to go. It was a social gathering place and a place of free speech, where teachers often met to engage in debate and to instruct their students. The court of the women also contained thirteen chests of the temple treasury, each topped with a trumpet-like opening and each dedicated to one of the current thirteen temple budget items. On the west wall of the court of the women, fifteen curved steps led up to the gate of Nicanor, through which only men were allowed into the court of the Israelites. The enclosed structure that was the temple proper contained the Holy of Holies, an empty inner chamber entered by the high priest on high ceremonial days. It was thought that he was entering into the presence of God.

Now was the time she looked forward to the most. She could not afford to purchase an animal for sacrifice, but she could add her coins to the temple treasury. She wandered from one horn-shaped receptacle to the next, quietly listening as male contributors made their gifts; for sometimes they automatically read aloud the inscriptions on the chests. She knew the cause she wanted to support and was rewarded finally to hear that one receptacle was labeled "Temple Maintenance." She stood back to let several richly clad worshipers empty bags of coins noisily into its funnel. Then she stepped up and with a joyful sense of freedom held out her hand and dropped the two coins. She turned and left quietly, unaware that one of the teachers had called his students together to observe her sacrifice.

## Jesus as Social Critic

Jesus had a deep concern for social justice and a particular understanding of the role of God's people. Earlier in his ministry, he had identified love of God and neighbor as the greatest of the commandments in the law. He had illustrated the meaning of love of neighbor by telling a story of compassion and unusual generosity on the part of a Samaritan who found a wounded man beside the road (see Luke 10:25-37). In Jesus' story, the religious leaders had not come across as heroes. They had failed to demonstrate a generosity of spirit that looked beyond self.

Read Luke 20:45–21:4. Why was Jesus upset with the scribes? What was the scribes' worst offense? What is the effect of placing the incident of the widow's gift directly after Jesus' condemnation of the scribes? What was Jesus saying about the temple as it existed and operated in his day?

Pointing out the widow's generous spirit was among the final lessons that Jesus the teacher imparted to his followers; for both Mark and Luke place the event in the time period between Jesus' triumphant entry into Jerusalem (which we celebrate on Palm Sunday) and his crucifixion. Luke also recounts that Jesus wept over the city prior to his entrance (see 19:41-42), lamenting that this major center of the Jewish religion, which had all the potential for claiming God's power for love and justice, just didn't seem to get it. Immediately prior to directing attention to the widow, Jesus criticized the displays of ostentation of scribes who benefited richly from temple taxes that laid deep burdens on the poor. Luke records a scathing comment in which Jesus accuses the scribes of devouring widow's houses (20:46-47). Jesus was harshly critical of religious leaders who pursued their own comfort rather than being defenders of widows, orphans, and the needy. Immediately following the incident of the widow's gift, when Jesus' followers commented on the beautiful adornments of the temple, Jesus predicted that those marks of ostentation would all be destroyed.

What a breath of fresh air the widow must have afforded Jesus. In the midst of his despair over a religious system that practiced luxurious living at the expense of the poor—a system that seemed to have lost the true meaning of sacrifice—he encountered a woman who really did get it. Her willingness to give everything to God without thought of her own need was in complete contrast to the attitudes of those who dressed and fed themselves richly and gave their leftovers to God.

Form teams of two or three. Discuss: Why was Jesus upset with the societal system that supported the temple? What would he have to say about prevailing systems in our culture? Where in our culture do you see persons or institutions emulating the scribes that Jesus criticized? Where in our culture do persons or institutions emulate the widow? Is the widow in this story a hero? What characteristics make her a hero? What specific heroic action has she performed? Share small-group answers in the total group.

She claimed God's power through the willingness of her generous spirit. How Jesus must have exulted in the moment! The woman's gift was not just a tiny offering to the temple but a gift to Jesus himself in lifting his spirits and a gift to all of humanity through its being recorded in the Scriptures.

The coins offered by the widow whom Jesus observed were called leptons or half perutas. They were the coins of least value in circulation during the time of Jesus. It took 128 of them to make up a denarius, a coin that was equivalent to a day's wage. Such coins were struck by the kings of Judea from about 40 B.C.

to A.D. and were hand cast of bronze (an alloy of copper). Each coin was uniquely shaped and slightly smaller than one of our dimes. Each side had high relief designs featuring anchors, stars, eight-spoked wheels, cornucopias, and other objects reflecting daily life. For the King James Version of the Bible, the translators—not knowing the name of the coins—used the name of the smallest coin in circulation in seventeenth-century England. In that version, the coins are referred to as mites (a mite was half a farthing). The phrase *widow's mite* has come into our language to mean a small contribution made by one who has few economic resources.

## What If ...

*The American Heritage Dictionary of the English Language* defines *generosity* as "liberality in giving or *willingness to give* [italics added]". Thus generosity is as much an attitude as it is a behavior. In drawing attention to the widow's gift, Jesus was not putting down what others gave. Nor was he approving of the fact that her gift might deprive her of a meal. In fact, as we have seen, he was critical of the system that had put her in such straits. Jesus described the widow's gift as "more" than the others because of the spirit of generosity in which it was given. To Jesus, generosity was not about the money; it was about attitude. What would happen if we could capture the widow's generous attitude?

Certainly generosity has to do with more than money. We can be generous with our time, our talents, and our energies. But we can also be generous with our money. God does not want us to leave our bills

What would happen if we as a church looked at the annual budget and decided how much of it each member should contribute monthly in order for it to be met in full and perhaps to add some new ministries? What if we made this determination before any of us figured our personal budgets? What if we paid our charitable obligations first every month and then paid the rest of our bills out of what we had left over? What holds us back from following such a course?

unpaid or our children poorly clothed and fed in order that we might make a generous gift to charity. But who among us does not figure what amount we can give only after we have met personal expenses that include entertainment, clothes that are in fashion, food beyond the amount we need to sustain us, and the latest toys for our children? Economic sacrifice is not a term that we Americans even think about unless loss of work threatens our livelihood. But then there is that widow....

## A Doctor's Legacy

In the popular TV drama *ER*, a few years back Dr. Mark Green, a man who had dedicated his life to saving the lives of others on a daily (sometimes hourly) basis, discovered he was dying of a brain tumor. In the final weeks left to him, he made a heroic effort to reconcile with Rachel, his fourteen-year-old daughter from a previous marriage. Rachel was deep into teenage angst, had done drugs, had a penchant for dating older boys, and was still resentful of her parents' divorce and their perceived lack of time for her. At first she resisted efforts at peacemaking; but as time went on, she and her father once again became close.

In a final touching scene, as Dr. Green's life is ebbing away, Rachel brings him a portable CD player and attaches the earphones to his head. She has found a recording of a lullaby that he used to sing to her as a child. Her father looks up at

> Can generosity be taught? What can parents do to foster a spirit of generosity in their children?

her, and his last feebly spoken words to her are "Be generous." To Dr. Mark Green, who had spent his life giving of his time and resources to care for the health and safety of others, the spirit of generosity was the most important heritage he could leave his child.

## The Happy Prince

In the biblical account of the widow, the generosity of her heart allows her to claim God's power even to the extent that she becomes an example of good for all time. Eighteenth-century author Oscar Wilde wrote a story of equally pure generosity that puts others above self. It is called "The Happy Prince."

In the story, a swallow on its migration flight to Egypt takes refuge on the way at the feet of a gilded statue placed on a tall column in a northern European city. The statue is called the Happy Prince, but the swallow soon discovers that though its sculpted face is smiling, the statue is unbearably sad. Its leaden heart is wrenched by the suffering of the poor and downtrodden that it sees throughout the city.

The statue is covered with gold leaf and has two sapphire eyes and a ruby in its sword. It begs the swallow to stay with it for a few nights to pluck its jewels and gold leaf and distribute them to the poor. The swallow agrees, reluctantly at first since the weather is getting colder. Once the statue's eyes are removed, it must rely on the swallow to tell it what is happening in the city and where the gold leaf is most needed.

Snow and frost arrive, but the swallow keeps distributing gold leaf until it can do no more. Flying to the statue's shoulder, it bids the statue good-bye and falls dead at its feet, whereupon the lead heart of the statue breaks in two.

The town councilors notice that the statue has become shabby and have it melted down to be reworked into something else. The foundry workers are unable to melt the statue's heart, so they throw it on a dust heap alongside the dead swallow.

At the end of the story, God asks an angel to gather the two most precious items from the city, and the angel brings God the leaden heart and the dead bird. God commends the angel for choosing rightly and says that the bird shall sing forevermore for God and the Happy Prince in Paradise.

## Of Statues and Swallows

The statue in Wilde's story had resources but no way to deliver them, since it could not leave its pedestal. The swallow had no resources but could fly about freely and act as a delivery system for the statue's resources. Both characters, in a true spirit

of generosity, self-
lessly gave what they
had in a relationship
that worked to the
benefit of others.

> What elements of this story are similar to elements in the biblical description of the widow's gift? What elements are different?

I have a swallow friend named Emalie who spends a great deal of time and energy claiming God's power by ministering to children at risk in our public school system. As she goes in and out among some of the poorest families in our city, she sees needs that she cannot meet through her own resources. But Emalie knows where there are some statues. Emalie belongs to a congregation of gen-

> Who are the most selfless persons that you know? Talk about acts of generosity that you have witnessed. Who are the statues and swallows in your congregation? How are they claiming God's power?

erous souls. She has only to mention, during church announcements, that a family needs children's shoes, winter coats, or Christmas presents; and before the week is up, Emalie has shoes, coats, or packages to distribute where the need is. One older couple who always respond more than generously to her requests live from day to day with serious personal tragedy, yet they rise above their own needs and claim God's power by providing Emalie with resources for the comfort of others.

### Closing Moments

Revisit the definition for *hero* that you created in previous sessions. After considering the account of the widow who gave her last coins, what, if anything, would you add to the definition? Work on rewording the definition, and post your new definition for the next session.

Distribute pencils and slips of paper. Relight the candles on the worship center, and dim the room lights if possible. Read the following invitation:

You have come to the temple. You are glad for this quiet respite from the outside world that so often is too much for you. In this quiet time with God, consider a small gift that you might add to the temple treasury. You might decide to give money to some charitable cause or to the church for some special purpose. On the other hand, your gift need not be a monetary one. It could be some small act of generosity or change of habit that would make someone else's life easier or happier. You might decide to give your spouse one genuine compliment every day. Or you might offer an elderly neighbor transportation to the grocery store on a regular basis. You might invite a new coworker to coffee with your group. Or you might decide to write or telephone a distant relative more often. Take some time now to consider a gift that you could give ungrudgingly in the true spirit of generosity. Write your gift on a slip of paper. Or, if you are not ready to make a specific gift, write, "I will pray for a greater spirit of generosity." Then quietly tear the paper into small pieces and place them in the offering plate whenever you are ready.

When everyone has made a symbolic offering, pray again the prayer at the end of "Opening Moments" (page 49). Find the hymn "Take my Life, and Let It Be" or the hymn "What Gift Can We Bring" in your church hymnbook, and end your time together by singing either hymn.

## For an Extended Session

Ask someone from your church's committee or work area on finance, someone from your church's committee or work area on stewardship, and someone from your church's committee or work area on nurture and outreach to meet with your group. Ask the finance representative to explain how your church's budget is built. Ask the stewardship representative to explain how plans are made to meet the budget. Ask the nurture-outreach representative to present information about ministries and projects that could be expanded if more funds were available than the current budget affords. Claim God's power by committing as a group to support one new program or ministry with funds over and above your regular giving.

## Intergenerational Activities

Read together *The Giving Tree,* by Shel Silverstein, or *The Give-Away,* by Ray Buckley.

Make banks for collecting money to support a local mission project. Banks can be made from saltboxes, coffee cans with plastic lids, plastic milk cartons, plastic soft drink bottles, margarine tubs, cottage cheese containers, and/or any other containers in which a coin slot can be cut. After cutting the slots, cover the outside of the containers with several layers of half-inch-wide strips of newspaper dipped in a mixture of half water and half white glue. When the layers are dry, paint the banks bright colors with acrylic paints and decorate them with paint pens. If the containers are not made of metal, the papier-mache coatings can be dried in a matter of minutes in a microwave oven. Otherwise they will need to sit overnight before being painted.

If possible, make enough banks for all the families of your congregation. Plan to present information about the mission project to your congregation on Sunday morning and to let each family select a bank to fill. Specify a deadline for return of the banks. Plan for a way to deliver the collected offerings to the mission project.

# Jesus:
# A Lesson in Humility

**Focus:** Jesus taught his followers that the prerequisites for heroic discipleship are a humble spirit and contrite heart.

## Opening Moments

Read 1 Corinthians 16:13-14, displayed either on a large sheet of posterboard or on a chalkboard, as your group greeting. As you have done before, quickly divide into five clusters (individuals, pairs, or small groups depending on your numbers) and have each cluster in turn stand and read with conviction one of the phrases beginning with a verb. Each cluster should remain standing until the reading ends.

*"Keep alert, stand firm in your faith, be courageous, be strong. Let all that you do be done in love." (1 Corinthians 16:13-14)*

Pray the following prayer:

Good and gracious heavenly Father, we yearn with all our hearts to live heroically for you. As we now carry your learning from this study into the world, help us remember to engage your presence in daily spiritual disciplines, to be always mindful of our identity as members of the body of Christ, to practice our compassion and generosity toward our neighbors near and far, and to do all these things in a spirit of Christian humility. Help us to be alert, to be vigilantly attentive and mentally responsive to do your will. Give us courage and strength to live out that faith in our daily surroundings; and above all, help us to love abundantly, claiming you power to make the world better for all those we encounter. Help us to live as heroes for you in our place and in our time. In Jesus' name. Amen.

## In the Upper Room

They were gathered for a meal; and Jesus, and perhaps Judas, knew that they were doing so for the last time. Jesus had so many things to say to them, these dear ones whom he had chosen to carry on his work in the world. They *must* understand. The legacy of the good news he had brought into the world and the entire

Read John 13:1-5. What, if anything, surprises you in these verses? What do you think the sentence "Having loved his own who were in the world, he loved them to the end" means?

future of the church rested on their catching—*really* catching—the spirit of his calling. If the content of his message were to flame and spread across the world, it would fall to them to be the sparks to ignite such a conflagration. And he had only brief hours left to embolden them.

During the last three years, as they had been his companions in ministry, Jesus had seen many indications that his choice of members for this inner circle of followers had been justified. They demonstrated devotion and compassion for the poor and the sick. They had conducted themselves well when he had sent them out in pairs on preaching missions. Collectively they had so much promise. How could he help them make the most of their potential? Tonight was a pivotal moment, the only time remaining for him to inspire the kind of idealism that would sustain them for a lifetime in his absence.

He had been thinking for some time about what he would say tonight. He knew what they needed to hear, but it required their complete attention; and therein lay the problem. Something in their attitudes, a subtle deference in the way they were treating one another, told him that they were not ready to listen with their whole hearts. And with a wrenching sadness, Jesus recognized what the barrier was: pride of rank. They had all performed wonderful works in his service, and each held himself a little above the rest. Sometimes on the road he had heard them arguing the merits of their relative positions, and he had been quick to rebuke them on such occasions. But the fact that they now all sat at table with the dust of the road still on their feet was a clear indication that they had not taken his words to heart.

Who are the persons you would want to have around you for a final meal? What would you want to say to the people closest to you if you knew that you would not see them again?

The host had provided water, a basin, and a towel for the washing of their feet as they entered the room. Rather than take turns carrying out this simple service for one another, the disciples sat proudly with dusty feet. Each one felt that to be the first one to cleanse another's feet would indicate subservience. Immediately Jesus saw what he must do. Silently he arose, took off his outer robe, and tied the towel to his belt. Pouring water into the basin, he began to wash the closest man's feet.

## Peter's Response

His feet itched. Peter tried not to think about it. The water and basin were there by the door, but the customary servant was not present to wash the guests' feet. It rankled Peter that this detail had been overlooked. In such an arid climate as theirs, the first rule of hospitality was to remove the hot dust of the road from guests' feet in order to insure their comfort. Obviously their host had presumed that members of the group would take care of the task for each other. James had come in right behind Peter and could easily have performed the ablutions for him. But no! James and John, those stubborn sons of Zebedee, seemed to think themselves too good to wash Peter's feet. Well, he would certainly not wash theirs either. Nor would anyone else in the group, he noted. At least he would not be the only one at the table with sand between his toes. None of the followers, it seemed, were willing to be a foot washer today.

There was an awkward silence as they waited for the meal to commence. And then the Master got up. Was he getting ready to address them? Oh no! With horror Peter realized that their leader and teacher had begun washing their feet. Everyone sat in stunned disbelief as Jesus made his way

> Read John 13:6-10. Why is Peter upset with Jesus' actions at first? Why, do you think, does Jesus say that Peter will understand later?

from person to person, gently cleansing away the dust and lovingly wiping each man's feet with the towel. Peter was aghast! "No, Lord!" he must have cried out when Jesus began to remove Peter's sandals. "You will never wash my feet" (13:8).

But how did Jesus respond? "Unless I wash you, you have no share with me" (13:8). What did that mean? Peter didn't understand, but the thought of not sharing in the life of his master stunned him. Passionately he said, "Lord, not my feet only but also my hands and my head!" (13:9). Again Jesus seemed to answer in riddles. "One who has bathed does not need to wash, except for the feet.... And you are clean" (13:10). Peter hung his head in shame. He wasn't sure why, but he felt that he had disappointed the Master and had just received a gentle rebuke.

> Why, do you think, did Peter cry out against Jesus' washing his feet? How do you interpret Jesus' response to Peter? Describe experiences you have had in which someone performed an unexpected service for you. How did you feel about being on the receiving end of such a service? Have you ever performed a service for someone who normally performs that service for you? How did you feel?

## WWJD?

When Jesus had put up the towel and had once again donned his outer garment after washing his followers' feet, he spoke words that anchored the lesson in their minds and that are prescriptive for us. Verse 15 rings a challenge for believers for all time: "For I have set you an example, that you also should do as I have done to you." Verse 16 makes the point of the action clear: "Servants are not greater than their master, nor are messengers greater than the one who sent them." As servants of Jesus, we are not better than our Master; and if Jesus could wash the feet of those whom he instructed, then we too are to serve in a spirit of humility that ignores all boundaries of class, race, social prestige, and political position. Verse 17 sets forth a promise: "If you know these things, you are blessed if you do them." It is not enough, Jesus says, to know what one ought to do. Blessing comes

> Read John 13:12-17. What is the bottom line of what Jesus is saying? What do the words suggest to you about being a follower of Jesus?

through putting that knowledge to work. In these three verses, Jesus was saying to his followers and is saying to us, "Through humble service I have claimed God's power, and that is how you too will claim it."

My friend Lilli exemplifies for me such a spirit of humble service. Lilli has a quiet, unprepossessing public persona, preferring supporting roles rather than being in the limelight. Only in her work environment is the depth of Lilli's heroism apparent. Lilli works in an institution for citizens of our state who live from day to day with extreme conditions of brokenness in body and mind. Many of the persons she serves have bent and contorted bodies and can communicate only in wails and grunts.

> Describe persons you know who are serving others in situations that you would find difficult. In what ways might we think of these persons as heroes?

Because they live in so desolate a human condition, most of us would be uncomfortable in the presence of those Lilli serves, but Lilli sees beyond the broken shell and finds value in each individual. She daily greets each one with a cheerful word of encouragement and maintains an upbeat spirit in their presence. As a therapist, her job is to exercise them to whatever extent they are capable in an effort to help them maintain or improve their functionality. Her happy greeting and her cheerful encouragement whenever she is with them light up what would otherwise be a depressing environment. In the true spirit of Christian humility, Lilli does not set herself above those she serves but rather tries to envision what Jesus would do in her situation.

The initials WWJD have been a popular religious phenomenon for more than a decade, appearing on jewelry, T-shirts, baseball caps, and even nightwear. (One of my favorite joke punch lines is "Well, for starters, I don't think that Jesus would pay $50 for that bracelet.") The symbol has been exploited until it is in danger of becoming trite through overexposure, but the spirit of the words behind the initials is on target with what Jesus was saying in the upper room foot-washing experience, the point modeled so

If you followed Jesus' example, what would be your choice of action in the following situations? Why?
1. This year marks a significant anniversary of your city's founding, and one of the celebration events is a gala evening banquet. This event will be covered by the local media, and the expectation is that the important people of the city will be there. Your church has received an invitation to participate. Six tickets have been enclosed in the letter. To whom should the tickets be given?
2. Your church has recently refurbished the fellowship hall and meeting rooms. They are now in pristine condition, and concern has been expressed for keeping them that way. You have been asked to be on a committee to draw up rules for use of the rooms and to decide the kinds of activities that may be held in them. Your committee has received a request to allow homeless persons to sleep in your church on cold winter nights. What should the committee decide?

well by my friend Lilli. The imitation of Christ is a central part of Christianity, and Christians must view every situation through the lens of Jesus' example of humble service. "What would Jesus do?" is not a question to be taken lightly. It is the measure by which we live out our discipleship.

## A New Commandment

Jesus followed up the foot-washing experience with an important message for his followers—so important that he labeled it a new commandment: "Just as I have loved you, you also should love one another. By this everyone will know that you are my disciples, if you have love for one another" (13:34-35). The twelve had decidedly *not* shown love for one another earlier in the evening, when their personal pride had kept them from washing one another's feet. After the humbling experience of having their Lord and Master perform that service for them, now they were ready to hear the words that would be instructional for their lives as they became leaders of the new church after Jesus' death and resurrection. But first they had to be humble before they could be strong, before they could truly love.

*Humble* is an interesting word in our language, deriving from *humus,* the Latin word for earth or soil. Gardeners appreciate humus as the vegetative substance out of which plants grow. *The American Heritage Dictionary of the English Language* defines *humble* as "marked by meekness or modesty in behavior, attitude, or spirit; not arrogant or prideful; showing deferential or submissive respect; low in rank, quality, or station; unpretentious or lowly." In true humility we are related to the soil, lowly and bound to the earth, emptied of all pride of self and pretension. In the same way that plants grow from humus, the capacities to learn, to be aware, to develop empathy and compassion, and to serve others emerge from true humility.

Choosing to be humble or to practice humility does not mean that a person must be a doormat to be walked on by others. Rather, the person who chooses to practice the heroic virtue of humility chooses the capacity to learn, to grow, and to serve.

Humility does not seem like an ingredient for heroism as our culture understands heroics; but humility is in fact the foundation, the *essential* ingredient for Christian heroism. Jesus asked his followers to emulate his example, and Jesus went humbly to the cross. As followers of Jesus, we are not so much called to seek great tasks as to do the good we are capable of doing in

> Discuss situations you know about in which one or more persons provided humble service that was not expected of them. What were the results?

our everyday life situations. And our accomplishments are not the products of our own power but of God's power, which we claim in Jesus' name.

## The Superhero Phenomenon

In recent years, our culture seems to have been fascinated not just with heroes but with superheroes—individuals who exceed the norm even for heroes, who have supernormal powers, and who can do feats beyond ordinary human capacity. We have flocked to motion picture theaters to watch the likes of

Spiderman, the X-men, the Terminator, and the denizens of the Matrix. Most of these superheroes are not earthbound and have strength greater than humans could ever possess. Some sociologists suggest that this fascination may be based in part on our feelings of helplessness in a world that we feel is beyond our control. In a world where airplanes can become weapons of mass destruction, we find escape by identifying with protagonists who exercise control through their own powers.

Biblical heroes like the persons we have been exploring in this study have one thing in common with fictional superheroes: They are exceptions to prevailing norms. But not one of the biblical heroes is heroic because of her or his own power. Rather, biblical heroes practice specific virtues that enable them to claim God's power. Practicing such virtues often sets persons against the norms of the prevailing society and also helps them make righteous choices. Biblical heroes remain firm in their convictions, often in the midst of suffering, and they are not always winners in the way the world defines winning. But from a faith standpoint, they are heroic nonetheless, and they set standards that God calls us to follow.

Compare the traits of superheroes in movies you have seen recently. What do they have in common? How do their powers effect a positive outcome? Is our fascination with such larger-than-life beings a positive thing or not? Why?

Daniel's virtue was obedience to God alone, and he lived out that obedience by continuing to follow the practices of his faith in a foreign land, even in the midst of adversity. Adherence to the dietary laws of his faith and to regular prayer sustained him and gave him the courage to face a den of lions. Sometimes our adversities may seem no less threatening than Daniel's experiences. If we are to live heroically, we too must practice spiritual disciplines that can help us claim God's power to face adversity with courage.

Esther had to remember who she was, to claim her cultural identity, and to stand in solidarity with her people. As she claimed her role in the community of faith, she was able to call on that community for spiritual support in making difficult, even life-threatening choices. Our choices also can be difficult. As members of the body of Christ, we too have a faith community that can support us and help us claim God's power in making choices to live heroically.

Four friends who brought a paralyzed man to Jesus for healing were members of a community that exercised the virtues of compassion, trust in Jesus, and tenacity of spirit. Through daily, small acts of compassion, they sustained their friend who could not walk, and their determination to secure healing for him in spite of obstacles was fueled by that same spirit of compassion and by their faith in Jesus as a healer. Jesus rewarded their faith and their tenacity of spirit by restoring their friend to wholeness of mind and body. Through prayer, acts of compassion, and determination not to grow weary in well doing, we can live heroically by claiming God's power on behalf of others

A poor widow's generous heart enabled her to give in the spirit of selflessness in spite of personal hardships. Generosity is a virtue that does not depend on how much we possess. We claim God's power by acknowledging God's abundant grace toward us and God's mercy, which we cannot hope to repay, and by responding with generous spirits that do not consider the cost. We live heroically as our lives begin to reflect our Lord's spirit of generosity.

Finally, Jesus was humble even to the point of accepting death on the cross. He taught his first followers a lesson in humility by washing their feet, and he instructed them and us to follow his example. We claim God's power and live heroically as we serve in the spirit of humility that ignores all boundaries of class, race, social prestige, and political position.

In one sense we *do* become superheroes as we claim God's power, for we tap into resources far beyond our normal capacities. Paul knew the phenomenon and expressed it this way: "I can do all things through him who strengthens me" (Philippians 4:13).

## So Now What?

We have been considering for five sessions what it means to live heroically. In looking at heroism through the lens of faith, we have seen that heroic living is not something that we achieve through our own strength or determination. Rather, we grow into heroism by claiming God's power through the virtues we practice on a daily basis. We are not called to seek out great tasks; we are called to be God's person in our own place and time, doing the work that presents itself before us. God's power is abundantly available to us as we choose to live virtuously and thereby to live heroically.

Consider the definition of a hero that you have been working on throughout this study. Is each of the virtues described in this section reflected in that definition? If not, write a new definition for *Christian heroism* that reflects these virtues. Does adding the adjective *Christian* change how you look at the concept of heroism? Why or why not?

As we have explored the stories of a handful of biblical personalities, we have focused on some specific virtues that might be translated into action for us in the following ways:

- faithfully carrying out spiritual disciplines such as Bible reading and prayer
- acknowledging our membership in the faith community through regular attendance at worship
- practicing compassion through acts of well doing
- developing a more generous spirit in our giving
- putting on a spirit of humility before God and our fellow human beings

Among these virtues may be one or more that each of us needs to rediscover for ourselves or to choose to practice more heroically.

70

## Closing Moments

Discuss: Out of all the biblical persons we have been studying, with which one do you most identify? What about that person is appealing to you? Why? What have you learned from studying that person? How might his or her example make a difference in your everyday life?

If possible, dim the room lights. Arrange chairs in a circle around the perimeter of the room, and place one lighted candle on the floor in the center of the room. Read the following invitation:

Let us spend some quiet time in prayer, naming for ourselves the heroic virtue of Christian faith that have meant the most to us in this Bible study and considering ways that we as individuals can claim God's power. Then let us be still, not voicing any particular petition to God but simply listening for God's guidance around these issues, trusting that God, who is spirit, will enable our spirits to choose virtue.

After several minutes of private meditation, return to the prayer at the end of "Opening Moments" (page 61) and say it together. Find the hymn "Jesus, United by Thy Grace" or the hymn "Forward Through the Ages" in your church hymnbook, and end your time together by singing either hymn.

## Intergenerational Activities

Ahead of time, invite participants to wear sandals. Set up a room to resemble the upper room of today's Scripture. If possible, arrange pallets or low stools around a low table. Have a basin of water and a towel by the door. Choose someone to be Jesus and another person to be Peter. Have a reader read aloud John 13:1, 3-10, 12-17 while participants silently act out the scene. The reader should pause appropriately between verses 5 and 6 and again between verses 10 and 12 so that there is time for Jesus to wash everyone's feet. The person who is Jesus should carry the basin and towel to each individual at the table in turn, remove that person's sandals, place his or her feet in the water and swish the water around them, then lift one foot at a time from the water and dry it with the towel, moving on to the next person after both feet have been dried.

For fun, have water play outdoors. Divide into two teams with equal members, giving each team leader a basin of water and a towel. Have the teams sit in two rows of chairs facing each other several feet apart. Have a race between the two teams to see which leader can finish washing her or his team members' feet first. For this race, the team leader must unbuckle each team member's sandals, swish his or her feet in the basin, dry the feet with the towel, replace the sandals on the feet, and buckle them up before moving to the next member of the team.